D1723993

ESPRESSO

Serves Two : 2 tbsp very fine dark-roasted coffee, highly pressurized water heated to 93-96°c. Approximately 40-50 ml each cup.

Caffè Americano

Serves Two : 2 parts espresso, 5 parts hot water Steamed, frothed milk for topping (optional).

CAPPUCCINO

Serves Two : 2 parts espresso, 4 parts very cold milk, steamed te a fine smooth foam. Chocolate powder (optional).

CAFFÈ LATT

Serves Two : 2 parts espresso, 6 parts boi Steamed, frothed milk for topping (optio

ADDRESS BOOK

CAFFE LATTE

ESPRESSO

Caffe Americano

CAPPUCCINO

Illustrated by Martin Wiscombe
Published by Robert Frederick Limited,
4 North Parade, Bath, UK
©2005 Robert Frederick Limited
Reproduction in the U.K. Printed in China

Caffè Americano

Serves Two : 2 parts espresso, 5 parts hot water
Steamed , frothed milk for topping (optional).

Name

Address

Telephone

Fax

Cell

Email

Name

Address

Telephone

Fax

Cell

Email

Name

Address

Telephone

Fax

Cell

Email

Name

Address

Telephone

Fax

Cell

Email

Name

Address

Telephone

Fax

Cell

Email

Name

Address

Telephone

Fax

Cell

Email

Name

Address

Telephone

Fax

Cell

Email

Name

Address

Telephone

Fax

Cell

Email

Name

Address

Telephone

Fax

Cell

Email

Name

Address

Telephone

Fax

Cell

Email

Name

Address

Telephone

Fax

Cell

Email

Name

Address

Telephone

Fax

Cell

Email

Name

Address

Telephone

Fax

Cell

Email

Name

Address

Telephone

Fax

Cell

Email

Name

Address

Telephone

Fax

Cell

Email

Name

Address

Telephone

Fax

Cell

Email

Name

Address

Telephone

Fax

Cell

Email

Name

Address

Telephone

Fax

Cell

Email

Name

Address

Telephone

Fax

Cell

Email

Name

Address

Telephone

Fax

Cell

Email

Name

Address

Telephone

Fax

Cell

Email

Name

Address

Telephone

Fax

Cell

Email

Name

Address

Telephone

Fax

Cell

Email

Name

Address

Telephone

Fax

Cell

Email

Name

Address

Telephone

Fax

Cell

Email

Name

Address

Telephone

Fax

Cell

Email

Name

Address

Telephone

Fax

Cell

Email

Name

Address

Telephone

Fax

Cell

Email

Name

Address

Telephone

Fax

Cell

Email

Name

Address

Telephone

Fax

Cell

Email

Name

Address

Telephone

Fax

Cell

Email

Name

Address

Telephone

Fax

Cell

Email

Name

Address

Telephone

Fax

Cell

Email

Name

Address

Telephone

Fax

Cell

Email

Name

Address

Telephone

Fax

Cell

Email

Name

Address

Telephone

Fax

Cell

Email

Name

Address

Telephone

Fax

Cell

Email

Name

Address

Telephone

Fax

Cell

Email

Name

Address

Telephone

Fax

Cell

Email

Name

Address

Telephone

Fax

Cell

Email

CAFFÈ LATTE

Serves Two : 2 parts espresso, 6 parts boiled milk.
Steamed, frothed milk for topping (optional).

Name

Address

Telephone

Fax

Cell

Email

Name

Address

Telephone

Fax

Cell

Email

Name

Address

Telephone

Fax

Cell

Email

Name

Address

Telephone

Fax

Cell

Email

Name

Address

Telephone

Fax

Cell

Email

Name

Address

Telephone

Fax

Cell

Email

Name

Address

Telephone

Fax

Cell

Email

Name

Address

Telephone

Fax

Cell

Email

Name

Address

Telephone

Fax

Cell

Email

Name

Address

Telephone

Fax

Cell

Email

Name

Address

Telephone

Fax

Cell

Email

Name

Address

Telephone

Fax

Cell

Email

Name

Address

Telephone

Fax

Cell

Email

Name

Address

Telephone

Fax

Cell

Email

Name

Address

Telephone

Fax

Cell

Email

Name

Address

Telephone

Fax

Cell

Email

Name

Address

Telephone

Fax

Cell

Email

Name

Address

Telephone

Fax

Cell

Email

Name

Address

Telephone

Fax

Cell

Email

Name

Address

Telephone

Fax

Cell

Email

Name

Address

Telephone

Fax

Cell

Email

Name

Address

Telephone

Fax

Cell

Email

Name

Address

Telephone

Fax

Cell

Email

Name

Address

Telephone

Fax

Cell

Email

Name

Address

Telephone

Fax

Cell

Email

Name

Address

Telephone

Fax

Cell

Email

Name

Address

Telephone

Fax

Cell

Email

Name

Address

Telephone

Fax

Cell

Email

Name

Address

Telephone

Fax

Cell

Email

Name

Address

Telephone

Fax

Cell

Email

Name

Address

Telephone

Fax

Cell

Email

Name

Address

Telephone

Fax

Cell

Email

Name

Address

Telephone

Fax

Cell

Email

Name

Address

Telephone

Fax

Cell

Email

Name

Address

Telephone

Fax

Cell

Email

Name

Address

Telephone

Fax

Cell

Email

Name

Address

Telephone

Fax

Cell

Email

Name

Address

Telephone

Fax

Cell

Email

Name

Address

Telephone

Fax

Cell

Email

Name

Address

Telephone

Fax

Cell

Email

CAPPUCCINO

Serves Two : 2 parts espresso, 4 parts very cold milk, steamed to a fine smooth foam. Chocolate powder (optional).

Name

Address

Telephone

Fax

Cell

Email

Name

Address

Telephone

Fax

Cell

Email

Name

Address

Telephone

Fax

Cell

Email

Name

Address

Telephone

Fax

Cell

Email

Name

Address

Telephone

Fax

Cell

Email

Name

Address

Telephone

Fax

Cell

Email

Name

Address

Telephone

Fax

Cell

Email

Name

Address

Telephone

Fax

Cell

Email

Name

Address

Telephone

Fax

Cell

Email

Name

Address

Telephone

Fax

Cell

Email

Name

Address

Telephone

Fax

Cell

Email

Name

Address

Telephone

Fax

Cell

Email

Name

Address

Telephone

Fax

Cell

Email

Name

Address

Telephone

Fax

Cell

Email

Name

Address

Telephone

Fax

Cell

Email

Name

Address

Telephone

Fax

Cell

Email

Name

Address

Telephone

Fax

Cell

Email

Name

Address

Telephone

Fax

Cell

Email

Name

Address

Telephone

Fax

Cell

Email

Name

Address

Telephone

Fax

Cell

Email

Name

Address

Telephone

Fax

Cell

Email

Name

Address

Telephone

Fax

Cell

Email

Name

Address

Telephone

Fax

Cell

Email

Name

Address

Telephone

Fax

Cell

Email

Name

Address

Telephone

Fax

Cell

Email

Name

Address

Telephone

Fax

Cell

Email

Name

Address

Telephone

Fax

Cell

Email

Name

Address

Telephone

Fax

Cell

Email

Name

Address

Telephone

Fax

Cell

Email

Name

Address

Telephone

Fax

Cell

Email

Name

Address

Telephone

Fax

Cell

Email

Name

Address

Telephone

Fax

Cell

Email

Name

Address

Telephone

Fax

Cell

Email

Name

Address

Telephone

Fax

Cell

Email

Name

Address

Telephone

Fax

Cell

Email

Name

Address

Telephone

Fax

Cell

Email

Name

Address

Telephone

Fax

Cell

Email

Name

Address

Telephone

Fax

Cell

Email

Name

Address

Telephone

Fax

Cell

Email

Name

Address

Telephone

Fax

Cell

Email

ESPRESSO

Serves Two : 2 tbsp very fine dark-roasted coffee, highly pressurised water heated to 93-96°c. Approximately 40-50 ml each cup.

Name

Address

Telephone

Fax

Cell

Email

Name

Address

Telephone

Fax

Cell

Email

Name

Address

Telephone

Fax

Cell

Email

Name

Address

Telephone

Fax

Cell

Email

Name

Address

Telephone

Fax

Cell

Email

Name

Address

Telephone

Fax

Cell

Email

Name

Address

Telephone

Fax

Cell

Email

Name

Address

Telephone

Fax

Cell

Email

Name

Address

Telephone

Fax

Cell

Email

Name

Address

Telephone

Fax

Cell

Email

Name

Address

Telephone

Fax

Cell

Email

Name

Address

Telephone

Fax

Cell

Email

Name

Address

Telephone

Fax

Cell

Email

Name

Address

Telephone

Fax

Cell

Email

Name

Address

Telephone

Fax

Cell

Email

Name

Address

Telephone

Fax

Cell

Email

Name

Address

Telephone

Fax

Cell

Email

Name

Address

Telephone

Fax

Cell

Email

Name

Address

Telephone

Fax

Cell

Email

Name

Address

Telephone

Fax

Cell

Email

Name

Address

Telephone

Fax

Cell

Email

Name

Address

Telephone

Fax

Cell

Email

Name

Address

Telephone

Fax

Cell

Email

Name

Address

Telephone

Fax

Cell

Email

Name

Address

Telephone

Fax

Cell

Email

Name

Address

Telephone

Fax

Cell

Email

Name

Address

Telephone

Fax

Cell

Email

Name

Address

Telephone

Fax

Cell

Email

Name

Address

Telephone

Fax

Cell

Email

Name

Address

Telephone

Fax

Cell

Email

Name

Address

Telephone

Fax

Cell

Email

Name

Address

Telephone

Fax

Cell

Email

Name

Address

Telephone

Fax

Cell

Email

Name

Address

Telephone

Fax

Cell

Email

Name

Address

Telephone

Fax

Cell

Email

Name

Address

Telephone

Fax

Cell

Email

Name

Address

Telephone

Fax

Cell

Email

Name

Address

Telephone

Fax

Cell

Email

Name

Address

Telephone

Fax

Cell

Email

Name

Address

Telephone

Fax

Cell

Email

Caffè Americano

Serves Two : 2 parts espresso, 5 parts hot water
Steamed , frothed milk for topping (optional).

Name

Address

Telephone

Fax

Cell

Email

Name

Address

Telephone

Fax

Cell

Email

Name

Address

Telephone

Fax

Cell

Email

Name

Address

Telephone

Fax

Cell

Email

Name

Address

Telephone

Fax

Cell

Email

Name

Address

Telephone

Fax

Cell

Email

Name

Address

Telephone

Fax

Cell

Email

Name

Address

Telephone

Fax

Cell

Email

Name

Address

Telephone

Fax

Cell

Email

Name

Address

Telephone

Fax

Cell

Email

Name

Address

Telephone

Fax

Cell

Email

Name

Address

Telephone

Fax

Cell

Email

Name

Address

Telephone

Fax

Cell

Email

Name

Address

Telephone

Fax

Cell

Email

Name

Address

Telephone

Fax

Cell

Email

Name

Address

Telephone

Fax

Cell

Email

Name

Address

Telephone

Fax

Cell

Email

Name

Address

Telephone

Fax

Cell

Email

Name

Address

Telephone

Fax

Cell

Email

Name

Address

Telephone

Fax

Cell

Email

Name

Address

Telephone

Fax

Cell

Email

Name

Address

Telephone

Fax

Cell

Email

Name

Address

Telephone

Fax

Cell

Email

Name

Address

Telephone

Fax

Cell

Email

Name

Address

Telephone

Fax

Cell

Email

Name

Address

Telephone

Fax

Cell

Email

Name

Address

Telephone

Fax

Cell

Email

Name

Address

Telephone

Fax

Cell

Email

Name

Address

Telephone

Fax

Cell

Email

Name

Address

Telephone

Fax

Cell

Email

Name

Address

Telephone

Fax

Cell

Email

Name

Address

Telephone

Fax

Cell

Email

CAFFÈ LATTE

Serves Two : 2 parts espresso, 6 parts boiled milk.
Steamed, frothed milk for topping (optional).

Name

Address

Telephone

Fax

Cell

Email

Name

Address

Telephone

Fax

Cell

Email

Name

Address

Telephone

Fax

Cell

Email

Name

Address

Telephone

Fax

Cell

Email

Name

Address

Telephone

Fax

Cell

Email

Name

Address

Telephone

Fax

Cell

Email

Name

Address

Telephone

Fax

Cell

Email

Name

Address

Telephone

Fax

Cell

Email

Name

Address

Telephone

Fax

Cell

Email

Name

Address

Telephone

Fax

Cell

Email

Name

Address

Telephone

Fax

Cell

Email

Name

Address

Telephone

Fax

Cell

Email

Name

Address

Telephone

Fax

Cell

Email

Name

Address

Telephone

Fax

Cell

Email

Name

Address

Telephone

Fax

Cell

Email

Name

Address

Telephone

Fax

Cell

Email

Name

Address

Telephone

Fax

Cell

Email

Name

Address

Telephone

Fax

Cell

Email

Name

Address

Telephone

Fax

Cell

Email

Name

Address

Telephone

Fax

Cell

Email

Name

Address

Telephone

Fax

Cell

Email

Name

Address

Telephone

Fax

Cell

Email

Name

Address

Telephone

Fax

Cell

Email

Name

Address

Telephone

Fax

Cell

Email

Name

Address

Telephone

Fax

Cell

Email

Name

Address

Telephone

Fax

Cell

Email

Name

Address

Telephone

Fax

Cell

Email

Name

Address

Telephone

Fax

Cell

Email

Name

Address

Telephone

Fax

Cell

Email

Name

Address

Telephone

Fax

Cell

Email

Name

Address

Telephone

Fax

Cell

Email

Name

Address

Telephone

Fax

Cell

Email

CAPPUCCINO

Serves Two : 2 parts espresso, 4 parts very cold milk, steamed to a fine smooth foam. Chocolate powder (optional).

Name

Address

Telephone

Fax

Cell

Email

Name

Address

Telephone

Fax

Cell

Email

Name

Address

Telephone

Fax

Cell

Email

Name

Address

Telephone

Fax

Cell

Email

Name

Address

Telephone

Fax

Cell

Email

Name

Address

Telephone

Fax

Cell

Email

Name

Address

Telephone

Fax

Cell

Email

Name

Address

Telephone

Fax

Cell

Email

Name

Address

Telephone

Fax

Cell

Email

Name

Address

Telephone

Fax

Cell

Email

Name

Address

Telephone

Fax

Cell

Email

Name

Address

Telephone

Fax

Cell

Email

Name

Address

Telephone

Fax

Cell

Email

Name

Address

Telephone

Fax

Cell

Email

Name

Address

Telephone

Fax

Cell

Email

Name

Address

Telephone

Fax

Cell

Email

Name

Address

Telephone

Fax

Cell

Email

Name

Address

Telephone

Fax

Cell

Email

Name

Address

Telephone

Fax

Cell

Email

Name

Address

Telephone

Fax

Cell

Email

Name

Address

Telephone

Fax

Cell

Email

Name

Address

Telephone

Fax

Cell

Email

Name

Address

Telephone

Fax

Cell

Email

Name

Address

Telephone

Fax

Cell

Email

Name

Address

Telephone

Fax

Cell

Email

Name

Address

Telephone

Fax

Cell

Email

Name

Address

Telephone

Fax

Cell

Email

Name

Address

Telephone

Fax

Cell

Email

Name

Address

Telephone

Fax

Cell

Email

Name

Address

Telephone

Fax

Cell

Email

Name

Address

Telephone

Fax

Cell

Email

Name

Address

Telephone

Fax

Cell

Email

ESPRESSO

Serves Two : 2 tbsp very fine dark-roasted coffee, highly pressurised water heated to 93-96°c. Approximately 40-50 ml each cup.

Name

Address

Telephone

Fax

Cell

Email

Name

Address

Telephone

Fax

Cell

Email

Name

Address

Telephone

Fax

Cell

Email

Name

Address

Telephone

Fax

Cell

Email

Name

Address

Telephone

Fax

Cell

Email

Name

Address

Telephone

Fax

Cell

Email

Name

Address

Telephone

Fax

Cell

Email

Name

Address

Telephone

Fax

Cell

Email

Name

Address

Telephone

Fax

Cell

Email

Name

Address

Telephone

Fax

Cell

Email

Name

Address

Telephone

Fax

Cell

Email

Name

Address

Telephone

Fax

Cell

Email

Name

Address

Telephone

Fax

Cell

Email

Name

Address

Telephone

Fax

Cell

Email

Name

Address

Telephone

Fax

Cell

Email

Name

Address

Telephone

Fax

Cell

Email

Name

Address

Telephone

Fax

Cell

Email

Name

Address

Telephone

Fax

Cell

Email

Name

Address

Telephone

Fax

Cell

Email

Name

Address

Telephone

Fax

Cell

Email

Name

Address

Telephone

Fax

Cell

Email

Name

Address

Telephone

Fax

Cell

Email

Name

Address

Telephone

Fax

Cell

Email

Name

Address

Telephone

Fax

Cell

Email

Name

Address

Telephone

Fax

Cell

Email

Name

Address

Telephone

Fax

Cell

Email

Name

Address

Telephone

Fax

Cell

Email

Name

Address

Telephone

Fax

Cell

Email

Name

Address

Telephone

Fax

Cell

Email

Name

Address

Telephone

Fax

Cell

Email

Name

Address

Telephone

Fax

Cell

Email

Name

Address

Telephone

Fax

Cell

Email

Caffè Americano

Serves Two : 2 parts espresso, 5 parts hot water
Steamed , frothed milk for topping (optional).

Name

Address

Telephone

Fax

Cell

Email

Name

Address

Telephone

Fax

Cell

Email

Name

Address

Telephone

Fax

Cell

Email

Name

Address

Telephone

Fax

Cell

Email

Name

Address

Telephone

Fax

Cell

Email

Name

Address

Telephone

Fax

Cell

Email

Name

Address

Telephone

Fax

Cell

Email

Name

Address

Telephone

Fax

Cell

Email

Name

Address

Telephone

Fax

Cell

Email

Name

Address

Telephone

Fax

Cell

Email

Name

Address

Telephone

Fax

Cell

Email

Name

Address

Telephone

Fax

Cell

Email

Name

Address

Telephone

Fax

Cell

Email

Name

Address

Telephone

Fax

Cell

Email

Name

Address

Telephone

Fax

Cell

Email

Name

Address

Telephone

Fax

Cell

Email

Name

Address

Telephone

Fax

Cell

Email

Name

Address

Telephone

Fax

Cell

Email

Name

Address

Telephone

Fax

Cell

Email

Name

Address

Telephone

Fax

Cell

Email

Name

Address

Telephone

Fax

Cell

Email

Name

Address

Telephone

Fax

Cell

Email

Name

Address

Telephone

Fax

Cell

Email

Name

Address

Telephone

Fax

Cell

Email

Name

Address

Telephone

Fax

Cell

Email

Name

Address

Telephone

Fax

Cell

Email

Name

Address

Telephone

Fax

Cell

Email

Name

Address

Telephone

Fax

Cell

Email

Name

Address

Telephone

Fax

Cell

Email

Name

Address

Telephone

Fax

Cell

Email

Name

Address

Telephone

Fax

Cell

Email

Name

Address

Telephone

Fax

Cell

Email

CAFFÈ LATTE

Serves Two: 2 parts espresso, 6 parts boiled milk.
Steamed, frothed milk for topping (optional).

Name

Address

Telephone

Fax

Cell

Email

Name

Address

Telephone

Fax

Cell

Email

Name

Address

Telephone

Fax

Cell

Email

Name

Address

Telephone

Fax

Cell

Email

Name

Address

Telephone

Fax

Cell

Email

Name

Address

Telephone

Fax

Cell

Email

Name

Address

Telephone

Fax

Cell

Email

Name

Address

Telephone

Fax

Cell

Email

Name

Address

Telephone

Fax

Cell

Email

Name

Address

Telephone

Fax

Cell

Email

Name

Address

Telephone

Fax

Cell

Email

Name

Address

Telephone

Fax

Cell

Email

Name

Address

Telephone

Fax

Cell

Email

Name

Address

Telephone

Fax

Cell

Email

Name

Address

Telephone

Fax

Cell

Email

Name

Address

Telephone

Fax

Cell

Email

Name

Address

Telephone

Fax

Cell

Email

Name

Address

Telephone

Fax

Cell

Email

Name

Address

Telephone

Fax

Cell

Email

Name

Address

Telephone

Fax

Cell

Email

Name

Address

Telephone

Fax

Cell

Email

Name

Address

Telephone

Fax

Cell

Email

Name

Address

Telephone

Fax

Cell

Email

Name

Address

Telephone

Fax

Cell

Email

Name

Address

Telephone

Fax

Cell

Email

Name

Address

Telephone

Fax

Cell

Email

Name

Address

Telephone

Fax

Cell

Email

Name

Address

Telephone

Fax

Cell

Email

Name

Address

Telephone

Fax

Cell

Email

Name

Address

Telephone

Fax

Cell

Email

Name

Address

Telephone

Fax

Cell

Email

Name

Address

Telephone

Fax

Cell

Email

CAPPUCCINO

Serves Two : 2 parts espresso, 4 parts very cold milk, steamed to a fine smooth foam. Chocolate powder (optional).

Name

Address

Telephone

Fax

Cell

Email

Name

Address

Telephone

Fax

Cell

Email

Name

Address

Telephone

Fax

Cell

Email

Name

Address

Telephone

Fax

Cell

Email

Name

Address

Telephone

Fax

Cell

Email

Name

Address

Telephone

Fax

Cell

Email

Name

Address

Telephone

Fax

Cell

Email

Name

Address

Telephone

Fax

Cell

Email

Name

Address

Telephone

Fax

Cell

Email

Name

Address

Telephone

Fax

Cell

Email

Name

Address

Telephone

Fax

Cell

Email

Name

Address

Telephone

Fax

Cell

Email

Name

Address

Telephone

Fax

Cell

Email

Name

Address

Telephone

Fax

Cell

Email

Name

Address

Telephone

Fax

Cell

Email

Name

Address

Telephone

Fax

Cell

Email

Name

Address

Telephone

Fax

Cell

Email

Name

Address

Telephone

Fax

Cell

Email

Name

Address

Telephone

Fax

Cell

Email

Name

Address

Telephone

Fax

Cell

Email

Name

Address

Telephone

Fax

Cell

Email

Name

Address

Telephone

Fax

Cell

Email

Name

Address

Telephone

Fax

Cell

Email

Name

Address

Telephone

Fax

Cell

Email

Name

Address

Telephone

Fax

Cell

Email

Name

Address

Telephone

Fax

Cell

Email

Name

Address

Telephone

Fax

Cell

Email

Name

Address

Telephone

Fax

Cell

Email

Name

Address

Telephone

Fax

Cell

Email

Name

Address

Telephone

Fax

Cell

Email

Name

Address

Telephone

Fax

Cell

Email

Name

Address

Telephone

Fax

Cell

Email

ESPRESSO

Serves Two : 2 tbsp very fine dark-roasted coffee, highly pressurised water heated to 93-96°c. Approximately 40-50 ml each cup.

Name

Address

Telephone

Fax

Cell

Email

Name

Address

Telephone

Fax

Cell

Email

Name

Address

Telephone

Fax

Cell

Email

Name

Address

Telephone

Fax

Cell

Email

Name

Address

Telephone

Fax

Cell

Email

Name

Address

Telephone

Fax

Cell

Email

Name

Address

Telephone

Fax

Cell

Email

Name

Address

Telephone

Fax

Cell

Email

Name

Address

Telephone

Fax

Cell

Email

Name

Address

Telephone

Fax

Cell

Email

Name

Address

Telephone

Fax

Cell

Email

Name

Address

Telephone

Fax

Cell

Email

Name

Address

Telephone

Fax

Cell

Email

Name

Address

Telephone

Fax

Cell

Email

Name

Address

Telephone

Fax

Cell

Email

Name

Address

Telephone

Fax

Cell

Email

Name

Address

Telephone

Fax

Cell

Email

Name

Address

Telephone

Fax

Cell

Email

Name

Address

Telephone

Fax

Cell

Email

Name

Address

Telephone

Fax

Cell

Email

Name

Address

Telephone

Fax

Cell

Email

Name

Address

Telephone

Fax

Cell

Email

Name

Address

Telephone

Fax

Cell

Email

Name

Address

Telephone

Fax

Cell

Email

Name

Address

Telephone

Fax

Cell

Email

Name

Address

Telephone

Fax

Cell

Email

Name

Address

Telephone

Fax

Cell

Email

Name

Address

Telephone

Fax

Cell

Email

Name

Address

Telephone

Fax

Cell

Email

Name

Address

Telephone

Fax

Cell

Email

Name

Address

Telephone

Fax

Cell

Email

Name

Address

Telephone

Fax

Cell

Email

Caffè Americano

*Serves Two : 2 parts espresso, 5 parts hot water
Steamed , frothed milk for topping (optional).*

Name

Address

Telephone

Fax

Cell

Email

Name

Address

Telephone

Fax

Cell

Email

Name

Address

Telephone

Fax

Cell

Email

Name

Address

Telephone

Fax

Cell

Email

Name

Address

Telephone

Fax

Cell

Email

Name

Address

Telephone

Fax

Cell

Email

Name

Address

Telephone

Fax

Cell

Email

Name

Address

Telephone

Fax

Cell

Email

Name

Address

Telephone

Fax

Cell

Email

Name

Address

Telephone

Fax

Cell

Email

Name

Address

Telephone

Fax

Cell

Email

Name

Address

Telephone

Fax

Cell

Email

Name

Address

Telephone

Fax

Cell

Email

Name

Address

Telephone

Fax

Cell

Email

Name

Address

Telephone

Fax

Cell

Email

Name

Address

Telephone

Fax

Cell

Email

Name

Address

Telephone

Fax

Cell

Email

Name

Address

Telephone

Fax

Cell

Email

Name

Address

Telephone

Fax

Cell

Email

Name

Address

Telephone

Fax

Cell

Email

Name

Address

Telephone

Fax

Cell

Email

Name

Address

Telephone

Fax

Cell

Email

Name

Address

Telephone

Fax

Cell

Email

Name

Address

Telephone

Fax

Cell

Email